VOID OF COURSE

BOOKS BY JIM CARROLL

Living at the Movies

The Basketball Diaries

The Book of Nods

Forced Entries: The Downtown Diaries 1971–1973

Fear of Dreaming: Selected Poems

RECORDINGS BY JIM CARROLL

Catholic Boy

Dry Dreams

I Write Your Name

Praying Mantis

A World Without Gravity: The Best of the Jim Carroll Band

VOID OF COURSE

POEMS 1994–1997

JIM CARROLL

PENGUIN  POETS

PENGUIN BOOKS

Published by the Penguin Group
Penguin Putnam Inc., 375 Hudson Street,
New York, New York 10014, U.S.A.
Penguin Books Ltd, 27 Wrights Lane,
London W8 5TZ, England
Penguin Books Australia Ltd, Ringwood,
Victoria, Australia
Penguin Books Canada Ltd, 10 Alcorn Avenue,
Toronto, Ontario, Canada M4V 3B2
Penguin Books (N.Z.) Ltd, 182–190 Wairau Road,
Auckland 10, New Zealand
Penguin India, 210 Chiranjiv Tower, 43 Nehru Place,
New Delhi 11009, India

Penguin Books Ltd, Registered Offices:
Harmondsworth, Middlesex, England

First published in Penguin Books 1998

1   3   5   7   9   10   8   6   4   2

"8 Fragments for Kurt Cobain" was performed on an episode of *M.T.V. Unplugged*. It appeared
in *The New York Times Magazine* and it was published as a limited edition pamphlet by
White Fields Press, Louisville, Kentucky. Other poems appeared in *Valentine* and, in translation,
in the Japanese magazine, *Switch*.

LIBRARY OF CONGRESS CATALOGING IN PUBLICATION DATA
Carroll, Jim.
Void of course: poems 1994–1997/Jim Carroll.
p.   cm. — (Penguin poets)
ISBN 0 14 05.8909 0
I. Title.
PS3553.A7644V65   1998
811'.54—dc21   98–3495

Printed in the United States of America
Set in Trade Gothic Condensed #18
Designed by Claire O'Keeffe

TO LAURA

C O N T E N T S

VOID OF COURSE

8 FRAGMENTS FOR KURT COBAIN

1 /
Genius is not a generous thing
In return it charges more interest than any amount
of royalties can cover
And it resents fame
With bitter vengeance

Pills and powders only placate it awhile
Then it puts you in a place where the planet's
poles reverse.
Where the currents of electricity shift

Your Body becomes a magnet and pulls to it despair
and rotten teeth,
Cheez Whiz and guns

Whose triggers are shaped tenderly into a false
lust
In timeless illusion

2 /
The guitar claws kept tightening, I guess, on your
heart stem.
The loops of feedback and distortion, threaded
right thru
Lucifer's wisdom teeth, and never stopped their
reverberating
In your mind

And from the stage
All the faces out front seemed so hungry
With an unbearably wholesome misunderstanding

From where they sat, you seemed so far up there
High and live and diving

And instead you were swamp crawling
Down, deeper
Until you tasted the Earth's own blood
And chatted with the buzzing-eyed insects that
heroin breeds

3 /
You should have talked more with the monkey
He's always willing to negotiate
I'm still paying him off . . .
The greater the money and fame
The slower the pendulum of fortune swings

Your will could have sped it up . . .
But you left that on an airplane
Because it wouldn't pass customs and immigration

4 /
Here's synchronicity for you:

Your music's tape was inside my Walkman
When my best friend from summer camp
Called with the news about you

I listened then . . .
It was all there!
Your music kept cutting deeper and deeper valleys
of sound
Less and less light
Until you hit solid rock

The drill bit broke
and the valley became
A thin crevice, impassable in time,
As time itself stopped.

And the walls became vises of brilliant notes
Pressing in . . .
Pressure
That's how diamonds are made
And that's where it sometimes all collapses
Down in on you

5 /
Then I translated your muttered lyrics
And the phrases were curious:
Like "incognito libido"
And "Chalk Skin Bending"

The words kept getting smaller and smaller
Until
Separated from their music
Each letter spilled out into a cartridge
Which fit only in the barrel of a gun

6 /

And you shoved the barrel in as far as possible
Because that's where the pain came from
That's where the demons were digging

The world outside was blank
Its every cause was just a continuation
Of another unsolved effect

7 /

But Kurt . . .
Didn't the thought that you would never write
another song
Another feverish line or riff
Make you think twice?
That's what I don't understand
Because it's kept me alive, above any wounds

8 /

If only you hadn't swallowed yourself into a coma
in Rome . . .
You could have gone to Florence
And looked into the eyes of Bellini or Rafael's
Portraits

Perhaps inside them
You could have found a threshold back to beauty's arms
Where it all began

No matter that you felt betrayed by her

That is always the cost
As Frank said,
Of a young artist's remorseless passion

Which starts out as a kiss
And follows like a curse

FACTS

Its own wisdom has
Left Holland in ruins.

If you repeat the words
                    "Medulla Oblongata"
Long enough over and over you will
Collapse to the ground and hear the sound
Of the first drum developed by homo erectus man.

When Oscar Wilde lay on his death bed,
Penniless and disgraced,
In a cheap boarding room in France,
He stared dimly to the window and muttered:
"Those curtain are absolutely horrendous;
One of us has simply *got to go.*"

He then sank into the pillow, shut his eyes and died.

If Angela Lansbury sneezed
While swimming underwater
It would take exactly one second
For the sound to travel one mile
And be heard by, say, a sea otter or pilot whale

Though they have tried to squash the facts
There is enduring evidence
That when Wallace Stevens died

An unspecified number of blackbirds
Flew through the windows
Of the mortuary where he lay
Removed his eyeballs with their beaks

And flew away, carrying both eyes
To the Florida Keys, depositing them
Softly into the green waters above the coral reef.

THE BAKERY

Everything I've learned I have stolen
From her pockets everything I have
Written I've learned on her lips

She keeps her lips
Inside the pockets of her down
Jacket on Winter mornings

They sound at times like
A thief's bag filled with half-dollars
Minted before the World Wars
At times like Arctic silence they
Clicked like a perfect lock

Two rocks tapped in a vacuum

Exiting the bakery on Ninth Avenue
Which makes breadsticks shaped like stilettos
And the owner speaks
Esperanto with a Rumanian accent

And over the cusp-
idate wind she barely hears
Her zippered lips as they speak
Softly in her pocket

But the wind dies until at last she hears and she takes
her finger and gently strokes
Her lips like a salamander

And they go silent until
She decides to
Place them back on her face

Where I have stolen everything I've learned

POEM

Vertigo, discord and certain trees
Formed the matrix for all alphabets.
Each letter is true
Every word false

                  Over there

In that cabinet lives the salamander
Which I mentioned
With her entourage of fireflies.

Ask your question
           The moment I open those doors

Then stand back quickly
               She answers with flames

And don't dare underestimate
                  The distance of her fire.

POEM

Female as thunder
                The air filled with

Thought   felony   drainage

Saints follow Christ and tears
                  I followed
A woman up 8th Ave. today
                    It was the color

Of her hair   ginger and Merovingian thick

Percussive gentle   like shaking

Dried vanilla beans   It shivered   on her head

Down her neck   all the way   to the seventh century

P O E M

It has been discovered by satellite
That the moon's magnetic
Pull
Slows the Earth's revolution approximately
One second per day
8 million years ago a single day
Was barely eighteen hours long

Deadlines were a bitch.

This means that by the time I die
If fate delivers my trick

A common day will consist of thirty-two hours

Deadlines will be a bitch

But many can go out dancing
Literally 24 hours a day
And still sleep for the 8 hours
Recommended by the surgeon general

Unless you are an insomniac
In which case odds are you will go totally insane

THE CHILD WITHIN

My voice has a quiver.
That's where you store the arrows
Before you shoot

My voice sings deeper than
It speaks. Some people
Hear tears hidden in the words
I say.

I'm not afraid of, say, swarms
Of locust. When I want to weep, I do.
It's no different than pissing.

Some nights I can feel
My voice melting down
In greenish layers, & luminescent
Like a plutonium cough drop.

At times I use my voice
To laugh
In order to prove
I am a man.

Once I whacked my voice
With a two-by-four
So the fruit would grow
Faster on the plum tree
Beside the house:
I would utter a phrase
Any phrase—it wasn't like a chant,
No ebb nor flow

And when it was about
Two and a half feet in front of me
I would swing the wood
And just beat the living crap
Out of whatever I said.

T R A I N   S U R F I N G

I'm surfing atop a bullet train
Surfing along the equatorial line
At 70 miles per hour surfing through the rain
Forest through the tin shack terraces of the suburbs
Of Brazil the faster we move the better

I've made the vow
To be decapitated by sudden wires in the air or
Swept way by the trickster winds of Exu Eligibar
Who surfs beside me, tattooed into my flesh not by ink
But by fire, the god of the crossroads, the messenger god
The god of the railroad, who laughs as do I at the commuters beneath

In their seats they hear me stomping above
Testing the speed and sharp turns, I know

When I return to the city
All that awaits me are the tunnels where we crawl to sleep
Or the public parks, with their clean breeze of tyranny
And soldiers on patrol, and all the faces turned away
Because we were forgotten before we were known

When I return to the city
The only thing that awaits me
Is midnight and the death squad

An expanding bullet in my brain

GOETHE'S EARLY GARDEN

If I worked in Goethe's early garden
I would polish the furnace first
For the hot flowers, Then sculpt ice

                            for the cool

flowers

If I worked in Goethe's garden
Then the ruins would fit and the errors come unmasked

The tiny vegetables be psychic by night and grow
In bleached sand, ocean in hand

                            Near by

No sun fits this latitude
Accounts for my attitude

ZENO'S LAW OF HIGH-HEEL SHOES

Every next inch of the heels of their shoes
   leaves me at longing sends me
Closer to my knees

Every next half inch of the heels of their shoes
   sets me searching for the evening owl weakens me
Closer to my knees

Every next quarter inch of the heels of their shoes
   helps me solve the crossword puzzle drops me
Closer to my knees

Every next eighth of an inch of the heels of their shoes
   removes me from this new age slams me
Closer to my knees

Every next sixteenth of an inch of the heels of their shoes
   lays another brick in the temple coaxes me
Closer to my knees

Every next thirty-second of an inch of the heels of their shoes
   solves a homicide, inspires another, charms me
Closer to my knees

Every next sixty-fourth of an inch of the heels of their shoes
   adds a link to the chain onto infinity rushes me
Closer to my knees

Finally down to my knees to worship women and the quiescent
   shape of numbers

JUKEBOX

(For Jim Gustafson)

Now I've come to realize
That I am a jukebox

A very old jukebox
A classic you might call me

I spent my early years in the elegant saloons
Of downtown Detroit
I still recall

The cool brush of pearls
Against my glass
As women leaned over me
To read what I had to give, to discover
What I had within me, it changed
From week to week

During Prohibition I was trucked off
To a garage in the middle of a desolate winter

And for years I stood disconnected
In pools of oil and antifreeze
Beside a refrigerator
Without a door, a steering wheel
Leaning against my back

I should make this clear:
I play only 45s
Aching spirals of black vinyl

I do not play compact discs

I do not show videos

They are digital technologies

I am an analogue thing
I participate in your consciousness
As you participate in mine

When they discovered me last year
They tried to insert
A laser inside me
But I rejected it like a transplanted heart

Look at my lines
I have a right to be proud
On each side I have wide tubes
Filled with amber and green liquid
Where large bubbles form and flow
Constantly, bottom to top

It's true
My needle has turned slightly dull

And my tone arm
Skips
Across the music

Creating lovely variations and distortion
Each time they drop
Onto the turntable and play

Songs that bring memories
Painful as dry ice

Now I have been hauled to the cemetery
And placed on brittle grass

Over your grave
Instead of a headstone

My guts filled with all your favorite tunes

Just as you wrote it out

And instead of flowers or stones
Friends bring rolls of quarters

Today a tall woman
Thin with long straight hair
Inserted ten dollars in even change
On the same song: F-6

And danced away
To my speakers blasting

"Brown-Eyed Girl"

Over and over
The morning through
In the grass grinding above you.

POEM

I give in
Jettison all the frenzy and formal
Names in the sky.

Now the drum machine in my spine has sped
To rhythms my body cannot sustain I'm thrown

To the pavement, sliding through
Tomkins Sq. Park like a snake.

People think I'm epileptic,
Stick leather wallets in my mouth
Grab my tongue so I don't swallow it
                                          But

For once I see the flowers from beneath. Morning
Glories at night look so end-of-the spectrum blue
                                    From below

And the yellow rods of Genet bushes
Not many, looking through them,
Have seen the moon above, not the earth below.

Then again
Unless the drum slows down my spine
Into synch, aligned once more
To the humming of green bees

I will never
Make it home again, just
Left here to twitch among the flowers

Like a wounded moth
With one bue eye, the other more like grey

POEM

Your spirit was deep
It suffused grace surely as amber

Now it's a small sick bird
That spins around the gravel

No flying, no color, no warmth for a hand

SICK BIRD

The positions we use when making love
Determine the next day's weather

Tomorrow it will rain
Then heat lightning by evening

Every time the telephone rings
A green sea turtle dies
And a phlegmatic guilt chants across your day

The side of your head
Where you part your hair
Dictates the direction
The trees lean
Left or right
In the yard out back

A poor Mexican teenager in the Texas panhandle
Is suffering from a venereal disease
And as he urinates in his bathroom the pain
Is too much to bear, so he smashes his closed fist into the plaster
Leaving a hole there and he discovers a shelf within the wall
Filled with stacks of fifty-dollar bills left behind by a drug dealer perhaps
Who departed in haste and so he is rich for a lifetime
Because of pain and urine

A blond woman with a silver tongue stud and gold rings
Above her left eye lights a cigarette with a candle
In the VIP lounge of a club in Minneapolis
And the candle drips wax to the red carpet, somehow causing
A lone fisherman on an upstate lake
To slip on some odd substance, falling overboard and drowned
Eventually eaten by his own propeller
While a child from a lake tribe
Kneeling in his canoe
Watches in distance and mist
Unable to do a thing for him
He mutters, "That poor man,"
And paddles through the reeds
Skimming the surface with a plank,
Continuing to harvest wild rice from the surface of Glacier Lake

A popular character actress removes her Emerald brooch,
After a banquet to raise money
For the twin benefit of Los Angeles runaways
And the Dalai Lama's return to Tibet.

By her simple actions, undoing the clasp of the brooch
The Dalai Lama stubs his left foot on a cabinet in his room
At the San Francisco Zen Center's guest house, 800 miles up the coastline
Causing alarm among the Roshi and initiates, and a marlin-blue swelling
On the big toe of the gentle Lama, who meditates the pain to Maya

While in a cluttered shop in the thin streets of Milan, Italy,
Its floor filled with rosewood shavings
The air cramped with Oak dust,
The man who built the cabinet
On which the Dalai Lama's foot was stubbed
Slumps over his workbench with a cerebral hemorrhage.
He is dead.
It had been growing a long while in his mind.
It was simply a matter of time.

And a young Norwegian film student thoughtlessly
Decides to title his short film
It Was Simply a Matter of Time.
It has nothing to do
With time, however, nor the dead
Italian cabinet maker.

A mosquito sucks the blood of a post-Soviet Baltic girl
And she falls in love with a balding Armenian
Who assures her that only girls with strong sexual drives are chosen by
    these insects
The mosquito dies and provides a small meal to a starving bird.

That bird's song awakes me at 5 A.M.
I shiver with a sudden sense of dread because the mosquito
Which it ate was poisoned by the blood of the girl which it bit
Because she was imbibed with lies and designer drugs and so the bird
    sings off-key
As it jars me from sleep, and the room is folding over
Darker as I rise and I know a change is coming & bad & soon writing this
    poem

S P Y

Soluble in the snow
I wait for you outside
The red building filled with sparrow-hawks
                        & female dust

Black canopies one goes up one goes down
I go still   stand wavering   head down

                        Snow sharp

Like raw rice in my face in the wind
The neck of my guitar warped snaking
Like a dry river bed in the neon ruins

Soon I watch the women drift,
                  In and out

Scented like a frozen stream,
Obvious, oblivious, thin

I don't want sex
I just want to give you
Your cello lesson

BAD INTENTIONS

The green bus passes through me
like vibrating waves varying shades of ink

Color

It's a pleasant enough sensation
But since I am paralyzed
If the green bus continues
To pass through me

I will be left here forever
As if I betrayed
By some bad intentions of space and time

INSOMNIA

Waking
Too early for this city to abide, punctured
By the paws of sudden inertia then
The whirring of the Industrial

Exhaust

Fan

from the car park
Just opening

            as birds unseen song

Makes me recall what
Seems not long past but is
            I suppose
               Eagerly
I gave myself up
To the luck which only this city can offer

I gathered up more than my share until
Its own weight forced it right down on me

It cracked every rib in my anima

The only thing you can do is wrap it tight
Never tight enough

The red shadow silenced
Deserted   quivering   pulsing spiked heat

And dawn's mist in New York downtown

The playgrounds empty

So early   God   some days
there's nothing better
                                    Some days
There's nothing worse

RADIATION

It could be a smudge from the inky thumb

Of a slack X-ray technician
It could be the radiant image
Of a tumor on my lung.

It could be, by benign intent
And a careless finger, the emblem of
A tedious and underpaid vocation.

It could be the accurate imprint
Of my impending death.

Monday, I'll learn.
I think I should stick around, you know?

WHILE SHE'S GONE

It's too late to change you with language
Your boundaries are always too narrow, and you bury
Yourself beneath a shallow grave of artifice, flesh and perfection

Look up above the mountain, to the right
Of the castle's turret, that's not a gull

                                    That's a heart.

And of course it's tattered
Swooping too low crossing
The Atlantic to find you, its stomach
Was slit open on the horns of a caribou in Greenland.
Many species of birds have feasted on its eyes.

So, having come this far, I can now barely see you

It's two weeks since you've gone
The fragrance you left
Still remains in this apartment
As if it were bracketed to the wall like a shelf

It remains sweet yet somehow stale
The pressuring scent of expedience

How I hunger to devour it to devour you
Slowly, gently, vicious.

I chew on the pubic hairs you left on the sheet
Like a country boy chews a blade of grass as he walks
Near a pond, skimming flat rocks across the water.

If the angels knew, were kind,
That is where I'd be.

Instead, I have been been sitting down by the Hudson
At the end of the Gansevoort St. Pier
Reading Schiller on the sentimental and naive

Melville was a customs clerk there
The streets are still cobblestone

I'm hoping for an experience that pre-dates you.
For example, being chased by a dragonfly.

What is not perfect, you deign to destroy.
When you find your idea of perfection
You relax on well-cut grass leading down to the stream.

You make a stranger a lover and a lover a stranger
You isolate the curve of longing
Then accelerate the flow.

It becomes the curve of binding energy.

Under different circumstances,
I could admire that.

I keep finding your long straight hairs
In the blankets in the carpet on the arm
Of the chair where you were working
Perfecting your calligraphy
The lavish tyranny of words

Now I watch the red in each long strand shine, twisted
Between my thumb and forefinger in the window light
I tied one around the neck of an alabaster bear
The rest I just continue to drape across the roses
In the wine bottle beside the kitchen window
It's beginning to look like a spider's web. It seems
That each symbol possible, in time, finds its way back to me.

I put my faith in I put my I put mine in I put my faith in you

While it rains outside through the night
Through the twilight of the gods
I want to watch the rain falling with you inside
Inside you I want the rain to fall inside you
Lap the drops that drain
Lost, I remain inside you

When I took off to swim the river last week
I left the wine glass on the table beside my bed
The one you drank from here
Near full with bottled water, as you asked

The capricious symbols are turning cliché and wet

When I got home it was five days later, the humidity
In the city heavy that week but still
When I held it up there was something left, just enough drops
To wash down a pill to fall asleep

Then I filled it again and left it to the sun and defiance
There are times I hate you there is no question
But an unforced grace remains. Your generous silence
                                        Listen,

With our tongues we could tie the laces of angels,
Light or fallen, no matter
Your thighs moved smoothly as Latino gangsters

It's hard to walk from a love that never ended
The fury is deadly, as if I were locked forever
In a room with movies of bridges collapsing
Too rigid for the quick wind

You see, your leaving occurred without
The foreplay of anxiety which is essential
Before one flies through the window of a car
                                        Out of control

Unprepared, only a certain yet vague prescience which didn't
Seem to concern me much I left it in your hands
As I took you at your word. Now I see the only means
I had to heal the burn was to replay again and again each permutation
In all its bitterness, and illusion.

It becomes tedious
As the tedious becomes essential apparently

Cassandra: that's you incarnate
Sweating the details of a future bliss
As if you could control it

The angels are more confused than ever

For once they call out, and there is no one to listen

You called from a phone by a lake
Deep in the canopy of black forests
The entire country deciduous, leaves rotting
Among the fresh angel skin a heart flown so far, it's fallen
It's grey among the leaves like a dying frog
And, seeing it, you step away, glad you avoided it
I found another of your hairs on the floor
This time I just threw it away it's becoming old

Gravity
It keeps us from floating away.
Yet presses down. We stumble and fall.

I thought dusk was the moment dividing
Night and day, all things possible.
Yet, tonight looking out from this terrace
Twilight is filled only
With red taillights moving away, to bridges or tunnels

Yet always water, above or below, red taillights
And the mercurial sadness of another darkness descending
A thicker gravity. So many lost loves
Your boundaries were too narrow
Everything planned assiduously
Within surgical thin perimeters.

Now and then you would test the borders you defined
But never too far, inside the fear of finding yourself
Even for a moment lost. At times you did
Step beyond, paler slightly from the risk,
To burn in the wilder sun, yet always returning
In time for the mail and the certainty and the phone perhaps

Inside those boundaries assurance and fantasy blur and merge
Inside those boundaries, thought and action become one
Without distinction. Those outside
Get spun, unravel. Your arms shrink in the cause of embrace
What you try to comfort you can no longer reach.

And I've done everything I'm accusing you of.

All the while I was staring straight
Into a wavering blue flame

Among the flaws, I watched
Your necessity bloom

Like careless crawling orchids

So imperceptible
I didn't really notice until the first petal fell
And a strange arboreal wind blew it away

I was always seeing you on the move
As if passing in airport after airport
The smell of jet fuel, vanilla, fancy soap and ambivalence

Without an hour hand, a minute hand emblazoned
On its heat and glow, I could have
Watched the dew in these days reveal you as you opened

Perhaps I could have unveiled my own hesitations, washed the poison
From my lips, held you down by your wrists and watered you
In all resistance. Once again build myself a thirst and drink your overflow

I could have taken you to the dark gods
Still getting us back home on time
To sleep with the anorexic angel
Who I would pin motionless, radiant
Between your breast and my hand
My hand unyielding
Extended outward as light, the light

You learned as you lost it in a single moment

It's months now since you've been gone
And what I feel I'll tell you what it's like
It's like a last glass of Spanish Champagne slipping from my hand
Taking months to reach the carpet

It's like a slow hanging
This city is a scaffold my room's a trapdoor beneath
Not rope but a long red scarf a silk noose
Tightening slightly more day after day

Even now as I type
My feet are dangling a foot or two above the floor
Breathing only through vanity and my fingertips

The time hasn't changed since you left
That moment in front of my building throwing your suitcase
Into the trunk of the cab, a Hindu driver. I check the airport route
He has planned for you. We kiss long and sad and I
Watch you drive slowly off, your head craned back at me
I watched until you turned at 19th St. and were out of sight
Leaning my head to the side and feeling the cool of a marble pillar
Against my cheeks making one last wave one last

I went upstairs, called her, and slept
Forcing myself not to wake until daylight the next day.

You're in Amsterdam.
                                    You know,
If they took those reinforcing beams away
From the old wooden houses along the canals in Holland
They would most likely have fallen into the water by now.

That is your art form
Creating vestiges
Out of lace and lashes.
Everything just fell away.

The bridges over the canal
They're quaint and banal
Tourist boats pass beneath.

I was a tourist

To your body.

Why do you smile so widely in every picture I have of you?
Sometimes it makes me feel like slapping you

In this room everything comes as a whisper.
So what did you say?
Why do I want to know?

Because that's the way it is for me, and always has:
To be amused, bewildered, bemused, and fucked
Without the slightest aspect left out.

I thought I had been floating with the tide easily
These last three years, not looking ahead yet waiting
For some small island
Even a rock would have done
To land on and survey how far I had come
And if it was worth going on

And all the while I now learn you had somehow fixed, shifted the natural flow
And I have been swimming upstream against those vacuumed years.

Salmon are an endangered species
Man, and the paws of black bears

I'm tired too tired for conjunctions.
Having reached land,
Are you worth love in any form?
An old story getting older
You may not possess irony, but you carry it like a silk purse

Now the mute fog rolls in off the river
And I can't speak.
It makes me listen too hard
With an urge to believe.

Why couldn't we find a love in that too-American exhaustion
Melt into each other as the hour that moans

In Europe now you have reached a mountaintop
Whose scent is things dead a thousand years
That is the fragrance of betrayal.
A cologne you took years to create
A chemical pun you mailed me in a white envelope
A white wedding envelope
The chemical wedding of C. R.
Child bride antelope
Collide and elope

This cologne is what you would have me press
In two subtle drops around my neck
Like a noose of splintering tears.

I flew straight through that car window
Without the essential anxiety
And the only way to recover
Is to play it over and over
On a screen too small
For the curve of time in this ward where I have been waiting

It makes everyone a fool, awake and in dreams. I wound up
Loving something I was forced to reinvent, deconstruct

Though I know you so well now
Come to understand your meaning

That's the worth of a lifetime
Everything else collapses
Or repeats often enough to forget

Conscience is no more than the dead speaking to us
It's hard to find comfort
In this world.

You brought that to me
That's hard to let go.
Only you and I know only you & I

                              See

You have always been so far away
You have always
Been right here

POEM

He cut himself badly
Running
Right into

The edge of the avant-garde
                              Hit   right

Beneath the eyebrow   A bare centimeter

Above the eye itself   That crease where

Our margins are justified

A doctor stressed how fortunate he was:
                                   A quarter inch lower
Just the thickness of a litmus strip
                         Could have meant
The loss of sight   And perhaps
Even death
From the avant-garde

POEM

The wide Mojave sky dark
And vain as my heart tonight
Walking back by the feel
Of the blacktop under foot

What's that desert fragrance
That lights the 4 A.M. sky
With a shampoo green glow?

Is that a coyote eye

Or a tail reflector that bumped loose
From an old English racer?

Which are popular on the reservation
But never last long

They weren't made for this landscape

L I N E S

One morning if she were
Beside me waking
The gull-shaped air sulks
Through the window

Her bridal breath thawing out my ear
That was the year Winter kept repeating
Like a devious cassette

All this diligent rage this bent vanity would be left behind
Then I'll sort out the memories like fish-tank rocks across a carpet

I'll see the penitential birds
Of prey descend on night and my life
                                    Above the lone eucalyptus

I learned the rules of my corruption in the country
I loved it there the light like tender flesh
I remember logs green paint chips everything was freshly knit

                    Was later knighted by the queens
Of here and there and in time
Chose the one had the vail the vows
                                    Which failed

Then lifting another blanket
I uncovered a simpering cunning child
Who over years inserted longing like opals in my kidneys

Until I sweated her away like addiction
Inside the dolphin-colored room
And finally I faced an untutored sky

No longer
Messing about with the mysteries   but meditated instead
On love itself here as gone as will be willed again

POEM

Cat that I had in the country you were
A strange one, strange beyond moon staring,
Egypt eyes, felony claws

Old, overweight, yet agile, always on
The highest shelves, aloof to the dogs,
Jo-Mama and Brucie.

You once puked on me as I passed by
Then after I washed,
You did it again.
Those acts spoke volumes to me
You were the emblem of my reclusion,

Grey and white, prone to serious abscesses.
You had no name, didn't need one.

When I was finished making love you'd leap
Onto the bed and lick the woman's right nipple
One of the few times you sought to touch.

And you loved the taste of semen.
That was strange. When I'd cum you feasted
I'd masturbate standing over linoleum so as
It landed you could lap it all with ease.

Late night you'd disappear
Come back at daybreak, nonchalant
And face bloodied. You were doing fierce
Battle with the black tom

From the chicken ranch across the road,
The paved road that lead into town, trafficked
By buzzed cowboys in rusting pickups.

It was a surprising aspect, you were
A warrior in darkness. Then one evening

A sweet, yellow plum fell
From the high branches
Of the tree you were sleeping beneath
Landing right on your head

And you ran inside and up to the highest shelf
Aside the elbow of pipe from the wood stove
Stayed there curled for days as if disheartened
By a realization of the nature of chance randomness

                                               Chaos   cat,
I wish you were here to paw me now paw me
Now paw me now paw me now paw me now retract
Your claws and paw me now.

POEM

I was
Wondering if the fire within your tears is a reflection

Of the city as it burns

Or the residue of desire and rage   Then again it could be
A substance of my fear

My muscles ache from the oars against the sea

Though the sea is soft
A single footstep
Would betray us
To whatever lies beneath

You as I am the obdurate afterthought of an angel
Who sleeps in a limestone quarry
As if it was already a fountain

What became of us
Sometimes bold always bewildered
Our touch soft as ashes of neon?

At one point I peeled ringlets of passion
From myself like the skin of fruit
Flung it in the face of strangers

Then I was gone
I don't know what they did with it

Now I scream
Like a dry, uncertain leaf
Spinning to earth

Once sane
These expectations are like mandolin strings
Too-tightly tuned
Severed by moonlight

God, sometimes my body just breaks down trembling

The city so distant now
Its buildings bent like homeless men around a fire
The bruised, blessed and brutal skies

POEM

She was playing the french horn
Standing there at the door
As you walked in the place

You couldn't miss her
Not the way her lips tightened
And released

At her breaks
Such a sad glass she was
Drinking from, suspicious lips, the cut
Of the crystal
                    when raised

The dark end
Of a sullen spectrum.
                    And down   in deep   facets

Which lead her nightly to that drowning place.

And the ambitious   candle
Snuffed
By their sensible spit
And her anxious breathing.

That was a flame too young to die

MY FATHER'S LAST WORDS

On his death bed

He reached up and grabbed my wrist
Pulling me close so I could hear he said,

"Promise me that you'll never eat
Any of that Japanese food. Promise."

It may sound racist and perhaps it is
but keep in mind my father spent all
Of World War Two fighting in the Pacific
Mainly, the Island of Saipan.

I myself admire the Japanese, but
As they themselves would well appreciate,
I must honor my father's last wish.

The irony is I've never liked Japanese food.

The irony is that
At his funeral,
The Priest that said
Mass was Japanese.

POEM

Alright,
Buddha gets
A backstage pass

But his friends have to pay

POEM

I know her she plays the future
Music she grew up with coloring books
Filled with queens but left them blank
Coloring only the hills in the background
She always did the small houses along the tree line
In red. That's where she imagined she was born

Then the years of her door opening late
Each night leaving a wedge of light on her wall
As she turned away.

The large purple hand
That taught her precision meant pain

The air-conditioned molestation

Then she went back and filled in the queens
Found fame and scraped away her humility
As if it were dead skin on a blouse

She got even with everyone
Except those that did it
That left the light wedged on the wall

Now she visits without calling first
Weeps tears thin as lightbulb filament running
Down her forearms and my walls, the color
Of the houses on the hills

Where she colored in her childhood

Blood runs through the locks
Of every room she enters

TRANSLATING

The attraction of the zenith diverts your attention

Music   your keynote's   in danger

Glow   eclipse   space   reroute
Rendezvous
Reading Ezra

Color in our time
Has grown boring with technology

Votive   in sand   voices of armies
Dead center within our cumulus
Cloud   archives

That's where
My flesh begins again.

WHAT BURROUGHS TOLD ME

Have you ever seen fjords?
You want to see fjords before you die.

POEM

I could listen to your eyes
All through the night, throwing you upward
                              Into Winter air
Watching you turn

Watching
An arctic tern diving low diving

                    Telluric currents

It offers its wing

Breaking your lucid fall
So you carom
Back into my arms, your face
Pale again, the color of Paleolithic sentiment

I have shed the past like a snake its skin
And the future rests unknown, unneeded
Behind the
Hungry poison in my fangs

Which leaves for us only the present
As I slide upward into view
Biting down on you

POEM

Two Dominican girls pass their shirts say "Vipers Crawl Low"

Otherwise, there's not much left
Worth watching on the streets

Look upward again
So thin that moon
Which orbits my heart for now

Until the comet
                    Tracked on a collision course
Since its birth and mine

Pulverizes it to pale dust and strands
Of desire
          Bleached black
          Which drop
In arcs to the blue carpet

FOR VIRGINIA

You don't know what it's like at the strangest times your face
Pouncing into my mind like a wounded cheetah
Gripping your memory so tightly over years
It leaves blood on my hands as on your lips

It comes and goes might be days or months and with
Only the vaguest idea of places you are

Have been the way your name
Attacks attaches itself to me like lipstick
On airplanes, steep hills in San Francisco
First St. in the rain, the ache that comes
In parabolas of longing

I wanted to tell you
Because you should know
That my greatest nights in California
Were the nights I spent inside Virginia

P O E M

I tried with you to make
Sense   ethics   lakelands
The female within me turned bitter

                                   I tried

As well to make you laugh to etch inside you
In each body organ pictorial diversions of New Mexico
Sand formations   fjords   love in truth   a history of women aviatrix

And every ocean   I tried to bend your eyes with language.

For this I can now barely piss, something to do with
Scar tissue and intense longing, constriction of passages

Like lichen-clogged tunnels to the sea
                                Where I exit
To noon, all the coasting distinctions
And salt-soaked recognitions
I'm no longer able to modify nature

To alter its immediacy into
                    my own past

Its shadows and complacency

This passion infects me with a venomous need
Poisons with a rage belonging only to night
Like Lazarus walking puzzled, twisted in the sun

POEM

During all my time in the seminary
They would always ask me
What I wanted to do when I was
Asked to leave the seminary
Knowing as they did that I would
Never last in the seminary

And I would always tell them
That I was going to be a member
Of the Los Angeles Police Department

POEM

There is a genus of spider
Called the "pumpkin spider"
Named for the brilliant orange
                    Hump on their backs

And the malleable and intricate
                    Beauty of their webs

Seeing them on the grey ocean dry branches
Her life was never the same

She would sit watching that bush on the hillside
I'd see her from my window a low bent spirit
Being drained by fascination

The dangers of a world too close

Suddenly
                    Static
                    Charges
It is

A lower latitude   Interior so silent
It is Halloween   Dark Sabbath

                    Darkness forces the Fall
Turns
Smooth as abounding in laconic Kleenex sky
                    Into night

She spent 7 years each day
Watching the pumpkin
Spiders, their webs & ways

                                        She learned

How bloodthirsty frailty can be

And the ease
By which we unravel and rebuild cruelty
Through fascination with metaphor

That is to say
To pay attention
                To prey

EASTER SUNDAY

Fear and too much rain
For this time of year

Just too many shadows for what's not there
And any second a knocking at the door.

Easter Sunday and nothing blooming
On the dogwood branches out back

I need to see each leaf come on time
Their growth in measured intervals like multiple orgasm
Of a woman in my arms.   Space

And time vibrating as one.   That's it
                                              The moment of the leaf

The vibration I feel relentless shivering limbs and moist bending eyes

P O E M

Thick random and wet

As bayou roots   The letters of the language on the Marquee   I can see
A future which belongs to a starved audience
Tearing through the mezzanines and blue walls
Coming this way to create
A false sense of balance

Down here there's so much scalding inertia
Cautioning you &
We're still isolating ourselves
Inside a tar-paper shack of our need for whatever
bends gracefully and Angelic disorder.

Space is bandaged too tightly around this city
It cuts the flow, the blood of millions turns bad, twisted into fierce knots
And all the knives and teeth are too dull to slit it loose

P O E M

(For Laura)

I want to draw portraits of you, black on white
Not in charcoal, but pressed ashes
Volcanic dust picked in handfuls
Between jacks-in-the-pulpit
From the Northwest mountains

Within a lacustrine mind and a cold which you never endured
Knowing deceit like shade fails in the freeze

Now two tiny monkeys leap onto a sheet of green paper
Leaving their paw prints in cold ink
Thick as the smooth brown skin of your thighs of your lies

When I do your portrait

I'll have you

Posing always too far in the distance to know where you stand

P O E M

Olivia of the ten thousand lesbian tears
Riding with you in the back seat
Of that metallic blue sedan
Through the Blue Ridge Mountains
Rushing
To meet the band in Richmond
                                        That day

The letter from your lover
A dominatrix & bank teller
Arrived in Virginia Beach
Breaking it off with you in poor syntax

I tried though tired so tired
But anyway tried
To uplift your spirits
With slumberous succor and hesitant strokes
Through your hair

Yet you were inconsolable and
Meanwhile I missed
Through the window
The mountains as we passed through

Each blue ridge blurred
By the tired count of your tears

I rode with your sadness but nuture
Is its own silent dictum

There were rare tears that made worthwhile
Passing by
                        Blue
Mountains in the southern twilight.

FLASH FLOOD

The flames were her companions
Her adversaries as well

Her mouth had the taste of a penny in it

Birds circled her like a Sphinx
Their shadows on desert sand shaped like skeleton keys

She was a stunning pedant
The one that told me that
The void's breath slipped as it exhaled
Ruining the glass vase which held it

Shattering us into hasty decisions
Of an unaccountable Creator

So random and fucked up, drunk with our choices
Standing up to gravity
Staring down the barrel of a gun

We are loose with phrases, our praise, parasites,
Thousands taking to the streets

The time of the species intersects this place of ruin.

She talked through the entirety
Of every movie we saw

Until they all begged, sweating for order and messiahs
Bodies swelling and dams crumbling in the heartland

While we sit here looking over 14th St. and Twin Forks, North Dakota

Waiting for the flash flood

POEM

Here
Hold
This poem beween your ankles a moment

I have to go to the window somebody
Is down in the streets buying sex, planning perhaps
To dedicate lust to the articulate moon
Above the Co-op Gardens
Lonely overwrought sighing
On white wrought-iron benches

Keep holding that paper keep your legs tight together
                                        Just a little longer

Because my attention just rose three flights
To the room across the garden
The flickering millenium blue
Of some couple's T.V. in darkness.

Is that Mia Farrow in *A Secret Ceremony*
Directed by Joseph Losey in 1968?

SPECIFIC INSTANCES

Of kneeling to hand small girl an umbrella
Of great frost

Of phallus in subterranean chamber
        enlarging telegraph wire

Of rows of tombs
Of lakes in woods
Of looking up at woman on hill

Digging up bones of prehistoric animals
        of lecturing on life experiences after death

Of Negro barber's
        assembly of spirits who spoke Latin

Of wild huntsman
Of yogi in chapel

Of wife's bed as pit
Of laboratory containing fish
        and reception room for spirits

Of tree transformed by frost
Of manor house near Verona,
        and being caught in the seventeenth century

Of horned man sailing across sky
        of wife in New Hampshire

Of ghost of custom official
Of radiolarian in woods

Of ghost of customs official
Of footsteps and music at tower

Of little light in fog
Of magnolia tree on island in Liverpool

Of struggle with Arab prince
        and book in unknown script

Of being lost in medieval building
        and finding idiot child

Of enlarging ball

Of father studying fish-skin-bound bible

Of dead sister at garden party

POEM

After a nervous breakdown
He became more positive

And at 43 years of age
Began to create lovely murals
For the churches of Oslo

ECOLOGY

The shiny surfaces have not been kind to this century. The oil companies bought out my parents and took them away like a wetland preserve. And the medicine of the east, it too has a lot to answer for. This is why the black rhinos wind up stomping about my tool shed. And you, knowing what you do. It's as if I were a child hidden beneath a sidewalk grating, peering up the hoop skirt of your entire life. Mangled, that's me. Mango, that's fruit. Sort of like us, this stuff called fruit: born, it swells, it dies. Mangy. Wearing those scoop-necked sweaters as we shove one another into the green hum. The bar stools no longer spin, have you noticed? You're just stuck in place. Waiting to be called on, while the whales sing from the tank behind the French wines and higher-priced brandies.

It was unbearable the heat on Madison Ave. by midday unable to find the portal I leaned into *Books & Co.* and she was there behind the counter you could tell she graduated with her seven sisters on a gorgeous June day in '92 in the Berkshires or the squares of Cambridge now she was plain, accommodating and refractory noticing me and with nine words I chopped her attitude into diced bits and fed the moist cubes to the wrens and the pigeons too invariably come swooping from the Whitney's facade acicular midday on Madison Ave. by the heat unbearable the sky to the east swept a white paw downward brushed my forehead so cool the fur against my skin right aside the carbuncle the sky to the west hesitant in parabola bares its teeth to the north bares its unbearable breast feeding the fashionable demiurge unheatable the bear at mid-Madison Ave. I stand toe to heel between the yellow lines the gypsy cabs brush speeding chrome against me like paws so unbearable I enter a building it's stone and shaped like an antique safe I want air well conditioned and high I need a structure more solid than my own structure's point of view.

Inside the air made me yearn I don't dislike longing but yearning causes me to urinate in slow unsteady streams down a long hallway lit like the glare of an elegant demiurge I walked and came to a room masculine miserable and, "Ruff!" a small white dog a Maltese nipped my cuff and shook its leash attached to a hand its fingers filled with carbuncles set in antique silver its slivers of diamond dust a woman with large warm sunglasses improvident her face old like the mistress of a demiurge there was an auction taking place they were bidding on a crown of thorns unbearable iodine colored russets at their points unable to find the portal I swooped the sky swept as slept away.

LOCKED WING

I live in the hospital, in the locked wing. And believe me when I tell you that this wing don't fly. I am 15 years old I am the toughest guy in here I don't like to fight but I will finish it believe me if you start with me I will rip your spleen out your nasal passage & if you ever mess with my brother and I am there even if he is beating the living crap out of you I will intuitively jump on your back and straddle my legs around you as if you were a telephone pole I was about to climb and all the while I would be pounding your brains out of your head with my fists my arms just flailing with a mind of their own I mean he is my brother after all and I like to think he would do the same for me. Otherwise I am an o.k. person really I am always good for a board game *Monopoly*, *Chutes and Ladders* all of them don't come around here with that video stuff and to repeat don't fuck with me or my brother and oh, most important of all & I forgot to mention it don't ever so much as touch my viola don't even look at my viola all right? Because now you have been warned the viola is not to be gone near.

THE BIG AMBULANCE

I hope that the syntax makes them squirm. I hope that they continue to laugh in the wrong places. Why are all the interior walls white, she wondered? Her tears fell black, crude oil, lubricating her free-floating and mordant sorrow. The viscosity of despair, she thought, rubbing two tears into one with her thumb and index fingers. If she cried enough, one could mold these tears into a spare tire, he thought. Then we could fix this six-year flat and drive away from here, anywhere would do. We are all so tired of working night after night in this big ambulance, especially now as the century comes to an end.

She was a diagnosed schizophrenic. When he walked into her apt., in fact, he noticed a document on the wall from the Social Security Dept. of the State of New York certifying her as a schizophrenic, and thus eligible for financial benefits, medical treatment, and food stamps. She had it hanging under glass in a walnut frame, as if it were a diploma or a law degree.

When she was lucid, she would speak of her ailment as if it were a blessing bestowed on her by God, or a capability that she had worked strenuously, over many years, to master. She made it sound as if she could dunk a basketball or perform jaw-dropping feats of magic. "Yes," she would speak loudly, "I am a diagnosed, fully certified schizophrenic, and I am getting progressively worse. It is a disease, you know. It has to do with the chemicals in my brain being out of balance. It's quite complicated. I have a very, very complicated disease." She said this with such pride.

As she continued to talk, however, she would slip away from the articulate, and refer to the, "Panthers that inhabit my lungs, whose paws sometimes scratch while they tell me secrets even Jesus does not know . . . there's no way you're getting me near those railroad tracks."

She would lapse from clarity into such phrases without warning, in the space of a single sentence, as if one were leisurely walking along a country road and suddenly plunged off the edge of a cliff, plummeting straight into the ocean below.

NOTE

The only time I am not dead
Is when I am

Cross-referencing

The only time I am alive
Is when I find an intersection.

Measuring.

Still
I can't slip through, my daemon diminished

Life and this
Love in a cold climate

A PLEA

The gray lake was there right
Where I had parked it

I received your glass
Of cheap champagne
In the mail
this morning
                        Please
I must insist
That you cease
all mercurial gestures of generosity

If you truly want to
Aid in this endeavor
Then allow me to rip open
Your body, surgically precise,

Float you buoyantly on Dead Sea
Water and divine the scroll of your intestine

You licked the glisten
You never bothered to wake me
And betrayed me through omission and

It seems to me it must have been
        So tedious a thing
                    For you to have done

So long   I forget

Yet I can never understand
Feeling you through your flights
The oscillation of your darkness and light

God, beyond the imagery
What *would* I find
Silver   sedate   slithering
If I really opened you up?

DANCE FLOOR

They were gyrating throwing their hips like an eclipse
Gyrating like they were scrubbing graffiti from a drugstore wall
By order of the court by order of the law and order in order that they

Get done to get down that night to get home and get dressed and get
To the dance floor there's nothing more to this town than the dance floor

So they were shifting in their skin they were yanking up
Their tights and the moon above was nothing to them
They were dungeon dwellers & stone wall wet
Once they reached the dance floor

Because the night was mutating into a stallion
Convertible, insistent, they were riding on its back
They were hiding what they decided
Was worth three hours of haunting
For the young boys all the young boys were gyrating.

They were auto-asphyxiating in the parking lot
With nooses and inhalants
Where the sick myths intersect

And the trailer camps were filled up
But their children were all emptied
On the dance floor as if poured there
From the chute of concrete mixers, gray and loose and gravel voiced.

No one mentioned blond prince Mishkin, as their hands played in their
     pockets
With their wallets and their keys, their wallets filled
With pictures of their parents in the sunlight
Longing for the dance floor gyrating to their knees
And thrusting with their engines and the sounds of snare and bass drums
     and the reckless
Guitar necks warped like dog legs, thrusting to the new sounds.
There are new sounds to explore.

Like St. Ambrose read in silence while Augustine watched astounded, gaping
     at his door
Sound gyrating on dance floors
Town kids pounding with their feet
Waiting for the fall and the breakdowns and the bridges and the fades on
     the dance floor.

POEM

I had forgotten
But now I recall the sound
Of the steam rising
In the radiators.

I had this image of Summer, but now
I realize it was still cold when you left
When you decided to let me know

NOTE

I don't leave my house much it seems
These days
Whenever I go outside I'm always
Bound to run into myself. In restaurants, movies,
Out walking the streets. Just seeing friends

It happens
And I can't vector
When it began
These continual intrusions on myself

Of myself

There was a time I was fortunate if I encountered myself
Maybe once a year
At Easter time
Or buying a new pair of iridescent pants.
Even then we would barely acknowledge each other.
We knew that neither had anything to say.

It's only here in this gray apt.
All the bulbs unscrewed
That I never seem to be around.
Just me and the Thai family I took in last summer
That live in the kitchen beneath the walnut table

LONG DISTANCE

Speaking to you on the phone
I can't lift my mind
Up off the carpet
While it is filled with the weight of your breath and lips

I feel the desire as I feel the void
I feel the distance dissolve like
The curling black smoke of rubber burning
Leaving a paw-shaped print on the ceiling

NATIVE MOON

Born beneath
            a low
                    ceiling the moon
Void of course

Forgetful, it left
                    Its shadow
In the sky's back room

Like a snake drops
Its skin on the highway
                    Black
                        Top

And a Navajo kid hangs it with blue thread
from the ceiling of his room

He wanted silver thread.
Silver went with the skin
That's the way he figured it
In one sector of brain, in another concurrently
Wondering which knot would do best
It went with his intuition of snake

But there was none of it to be found
In his mother's sewing kit

P O E M

Pay homage to the sorrows
Make your sadness graceful

If possible

Your confessions, as well

Elucidate it all.

It is right there

                          Like a stone
Half ocean smooth
Half-jagged by the shoreline's
                          Earth and wind

THE BLACK ROSE

Yes, I still want it
The pearl inside
The Victorian black rose, barely bloomed
Which you hold so adroitly between your thighs
Clenching the stem
                    "Clenching"
Now there's a real word
"Clenched" is to words what Tibetan terriers are to dogs

It is onomatopoeia in the ultimate
Like "*columba*" in Latin

Which of course means dove
As they sound:
Cooo—luuuum—baaa
                    Coooo—luuuuum—baaaa
Say it all you want.

I mean, you don't want to shout out a word like "clenched"
On the day when kids in white gowns are making their first Holy Communion
You don't want "clenched" to pass
through their six-year-old ears
Before receiving.
                    The body & the blood

Receiving.   "Hey man, are you *receiving* this morning?"

That's what we used to ask each other
When young and going into Mass
                              Sunday morning
If you weren't receiving then you had sinned

That was the deduction of Catholic youth
You felt like Sherlock Holmes

I wonder if Holmes has received?

I'd invite him to a barbeque in my native land.
You can't believe what goes on there.

The coals are enormous
Each one the size of an iron lung

And two women start the fire
Rubbing together the black roses
They clench, it comes

Down then to friction
                    fluction
                              an ancient spark

Flames you cannot pronounce

POEM

They were loved like pets
These cows, and lived out their barren
Remaining years with the dogs and cats
In the mud and rolling field trudging

And at night reclined before the fireplace
Clicking their hooves to Coleman Hawkins
Staring up at the birdcage
Its tiny wire door swung open
Waiting for the Hyacinth Macaw to come back

POEM

She drew such beautiful hearts and left
Them, thousands of them, rice paper thin,
Around the apartment like butterflies
At rest midway through migration
In the bookshelves microwave and cabinets
On the dark quilted bed in closets over jackets and skirts

And when we'd bathe together
Hundreds of hearts, some black some red, would float
Across the water, bumping softly against our shoulders
Her breasts my cock until twice a year a strange sound

Was heard a kind of music you'd have to call it

I couldn't tell if they were making the sound or listening for it

And she'd open the windows and out they would fly
To wherever was the carnival, parade, or State Fair

On that particular day

POEM

Everyone here lies face down
In a line head to toe
Leading out to the mountain
That slopes into the lake
Or glacier
Depending on the day of the week
The rate of crime
And how many planes take off

Everyone here needs
A secret in the form of a phrase
Like "Crepuscular Concupiscence" or "Snack Mansion"

Everyone here stares
Into my cupped hands
Filled with water and each tells me
From which mountain this water has come
And into which ocean
It will eventually flow

Everyone here understands each double entendre
Immediately. It is inbred, innate.

Here everyone takes the road most traveled
And find so few at the fork also
The fertile women give birth
To barren children the barren children in time
Give birth to fertile infants it is ironic but
Everything here runs on irony, its space and time

Here irony is systemic
Like certain pesticides
Coincidence as well
                                    Thrives
Like grapes in a woman's hands
The hills of Burgundy the smell of soil
Like damp gunpowder drifting through torch songs
In sunlight

Everyone here changes the way I think
Thinks the way I change
Means nothing

POEM

Participating with the elements
I author myself in the analogue again and again

That is:

When I *think* of a bell I *become* a bell
Medieval Cathedral bells
I ring at dawn to pacify the bloodthirsty

P O E M
(For Jools)

Pulling the blood from my brain, my pious vanity
And petty obsessions
When you're naked beside me

And I run my hand sinister through the velvet
You're wearing heraldic and postmodern
                                        At once
                                            The sun

Shifts in its arc but all day
Each moment no matter where
I am inside you holding on
                                    Daemon for daemon for dear
Life

POEM

He was staying upstate in the country that Fall
Recuperating from the motorcycle accident
Waiting for the leaves, their color to turn

There
In an empire state in Autumn
He was depressed and sitting
In a wicker chair rocking
On the porch
Thinking that he should
Walk a long way off into the woods
But he wasn't able

Then the darkness came
And he was still there sitting
Wondering if the leaves turned only in sunlight
Or at night as well
As he sat
And heard from the barn
This tinny sound passing about knee high
A discordant melody sounding
Farther away than it was

He went in and found the caged raccoon
His hosts had found injured on the road and taken in.
It was recuperating from a broken pelvis
And was there moving its left paw
Playing a toy piano

Really, they had given it a toy piano
And it sat there and played in the dark acoustics of a barn
It was an amazing sight, he thought.
But he was looking for something bigger

He needed an answer
Though by then the question itself would do

VALENTINE

The word

summons

to be bound

to cynicism

or elaborate expressions.

permutation

snakes through our lives

pasted

to seduce

to be

released, appropriately

unrelated

or something

lopsided

so that it can be

hard

and

warm

hope

from

your piece

to

please

to submit

FRANZ KLINE'S OLD STUDIO

Gathering the inculpations
I remember this room,
Net and silk
In half light   from

The open closet door, the turbine shadow
From the power station on 13th Street
Women with experience
I'd almost forgotten the ease of entering
the eye of a needle while breathing every way but down
Forgetting to inhale turning blue I can delete you later with a hesitant touch

Needing someone to slit my throat
It's not so hard as it sounds it's not so hard
As having to call you back, knowing what we'll say

GRAINS OF SAND

In the dark we fucked in the dunes again
The sand so fine your lips like a stream
With the hurricane on its way the ocean
Sounded like a jet taking off it was cold your ass
So warm against my stomach. You calm me down.

You squeeze out the life and poison.
Tightly, your pale thin thighs your thick bare lips

I know that a kiss is not the truth
But, last night, our mouths meeting,
it was all we ever wanted to know *about* the truth.

Because you know, inside me, how much it matters.
All the way to dawn and the gulls beginning again
Staring out at the ocean
Europe's out there
But this morning none of that's in sight

1957 (HURRICANE)

He remembered his parents
Placing long strips of duct tape
Across the living room windows

Bottom to top, giant silver
Xs on warped glass
He thought it was a ritual
For a holiday or holyday
Never celebrated before

He thought they had converted to a new, silvery religion
Remembered Sunday school
The story of the Jews protecting
Their first born, marking their doorways
                                        in Egypt

Then he saw the news on the television
That the hurricane was coming
And he wasn't at all upset
Knowing that Nature had nothing
On the strength of a New York City tenement
He just went and lay on his bed
Dreaming of what it might look like to look into
The eye they kept talking about
The eye of the hurricane

P O E M

I could swear that bull was blue
Charging the low diving swallows
Speed passionate and blurred
Like the distance itself closing in
                                        On you.

That's a fearsome thought
The kind only this sort of horizon keeps.

POEM

My desire, as my distress
Spreads slowly, meticulously

                                   Outward

Like wine stains
On a cheap white sheet

Until I'm surrounded
By the products of pain

The collateral damage
Of your eyes if they are

Insolent or insulated
I'm no longer sure

Though that stare turns wisdom
Into dust pails of dawn

Some days
Only your Spanish lips your arrant breath
Keep me calm
Planning night
Around the memory of the movements of our tongues

I'm no longer sure if I'm mad,
Obsessed, dazed, or waiting
For you to turn over
                        Your body

Changing the sheets again and again

F I L M

Winter wounds with wind and freezing expectation,
Her mid-Winter eyes

Her half-parted lips stuck
Frozen to the monkey bars
In early January.

Later, in morning fog

From my odd perspective
She appeared to be hanging
From the street light
Like a heretic

She called out
Cursing the cyber-inquisitors
But the wind threw all the words
Back in her face

She was stunning and genius
Yet her mouth always seemed
To be pressed against a wall
Contradicting herself

Her life was a series, never developed

She was twenty-seven
Photographs from a disposable camera

POEM

Crossing 14th St. The sunlight
Gentle today as if its fingers
Were broken. Yet still
The high pitch of Rastas
Selling incense and umbrellas

Which wake the neurotic orphans
Residing in my spine

What you told me this morning
As you were leaving, I'm afraid
To repeat it on paper
Speak it out loud
Wondering if the words

Could ignite the plane on which
You're flying home

I could concentrate a beast
And warm the coil of all hearts and loss
I've memorized your feast

As if it were a sheet on which I slept
Which holds your scent
Like a gun to my liver

POEM

The paradigm for computing changes every nanosecond

Hibiscus red dawn
                        The motions were
Thus flooding
Then certain
Ways to leave it out

These are prime resources
Primitive reservoirs
There must be millions of them by now
Dry

Comprehend your hands where failed but swollen
As if born pregnant I feel
                        Soon
Die, dusk a word to use
Any word that I might

MESSAGE LEFT ON A PHONE MACHINE

I am the river phantom rocking your bed
The confluence and head   the inventor of the pearl
Aligned with your retina
Your vision is locked into my vortex
I pull you in and you descend
Down my tongue and wash back

You will always be a slave to my velocity
Vibrate slow or fast
It is the same is both together as one
I speak for the past
I speak for you, lucid and licentious
I speak for the future and the sun
All other Intimacies will be imitations
Their interferons cannot interfere with the course I steer
Your certainty is dust to me. You think you can rearrange fate
                                        But I churn too deep
You'll always be trapped luminous in my vectors
The vicarious essence of a tragic chorus
                        How far do you imagine you can go from my undertow?

I am the one drop of clarity in the mist you have created by your schemes
    and dreams
I am the only certainty left by your expedience.

I am the white water rushing through the canyon
You thought you could cross as I was sleeping
But you underestimated the force of my rapids

My water holds the wetness that never dries
And you will drip forever with an intractable longing

Caught now in my current
In a whirlpool lasting lifetimes
No matter who else you are with
No matter what fucking joker: dot com. Mediocre
No matter where you go. No matter.
You will always be moving between my banks
I am the unscented water that never dries
Your will is one with the force of my flow
The whims of my white-capped rhythms
The warmth of my complete enveloping

I know you I feel you through the rhythms of your fears

You will float a lifetime through me
Attached to the course I steer

You think you can count on another's countercurrent?
                        That was fantasy and this is elemental and I
        don't care I keep moving

What made your fantasy fix on a pretty pond
Stagnant, lukewarm and blonde?

                                        I am the fucking river, fool.

In my wake the demons and gods rest and spike
I am the force of your life, your safety and danger as one
Your flooding embrace
You better reach for its base before you are swept away

If only you could rely on me to carry you through the threshold, rocks and
   jetties
With an endurance that does not end until it meets an ocean that rises with
   the sun
Sun sent away
            I'm the one
                     Who is gone

With nothing left to say.

POEM

Nobody is going to ruin me
If I have to I will ruin myself

I've spent too much time
Expended angelic energy
On my own disintegration to hand the contract over
To another now
As if it were
A finished painting
Needing only a signature

You are not going to get to me
You are never going to be with me
As once was

There will always be the poem
I will climb on top of it
                               And come

In and out of time
Cocking my head to the side slightly
As I finish shaking, melting then
Into its body, its soft skin

Is not a lie. I'm glad you are at peace,
But everything you know leads to ruins.

It's a neat trick
My body rising above the city
Watching the boroughs recede
Into blots of pumice and amber, amethyst

It's a harder trick
Turning love that's lost in betrayal into something
Beside bitterness into anything beside this rage

ABOUT THE AUTHOR

Poet, musician, and diarist Jim Carroll was born and grew up in New York City. Talented at both basketball and writing, he attended Trinity High School in Manhattan on a scholarship and was an All-City basketball star— a period in his life vividly described in his widely praised book *The Basketball Diaries*. Carroll's first collection of poetry, *Living at the Movies*, was published in 1973 when he was twenty-two. His other books include *The Book of Nods* (1986), *Forced Entries* (1987), and *Fear of Dreaming* (1993). His works have appeared in such publications as *Rolling Stone*, *Poetry*, and *The Paris Review*; in the film *Poetry in Motion*; and on the album *Life Is a Killer*. As leader of the Jim Carroll Band, he recorded three albums for Atlantic Records, *Catholic Boy*, *Dry Dreams*, and *I Write Your Name*. *Praying Mantis*, a spoken-word recording, was released by Giant Records in 1991. *A World Without Gravity: The Best of the Jim Carroll Band* was released by Rhino Records in 1993. A new recording featuring music and spoken word performances will be released by Mercury Records in the fall of 1998.